Things To Think About

A Collection Of Poems

Areeth Shah

Made with ❤ on the BookLeaf Publishing Platform
www.bookleafpub.in
www.bookleafpub.com

Dedication

To all who cannot find words to express their thoughts. To the moments in life where you find the real beauty of life, existence and poetry. To the moments of happiness, joy, grief, anger, and thought.

Preface

"Things To Think About" was born from the embers left by the fire of thought, philosophy, and love. It consists of a collection of poems that not only represent the poet's thoughts but also represent the thoughts and ideas that people may have but are not able to fully express. While glancing through the titles of the poems, one may realize that these poems are on a wide array of topics, from Love, to War, to Life, to Memories, and countless more. Through his poems, the poet encourages one and all to traverse the path of literature and poetry, and express their ideas, thoughts, and philosophies though , the art that is poetry. He is a firm believer of the statement, " We don't read and write poetry because it's cute. We read and write poetry because we are members of the human race. And the human race is filled with passion. And medicine, law, business, engineering, these are noble pursuits and necessary to sustain life. But poetry, beauty, romance, love, these are what we stay alive for." - Robin Williams (As John Keating, in the Dead Poets Society), and has written this book, following this as his guiding principles. Let this be a reminder to strive for excellence, and do what you want.

Acknowledgements

I would like to extend my gratitude to my Mother, Mrs. Purna Shah, and my Father, Mr. Hemanshu Shah, who have always been there for me, guiding me through life, and always being there for me through thick and thin. I would also like to thank God for giving me such loving parents, and amazing opportunities throughout my life. Thirdly, I would like to thank all who have been there from the start. Lastly, I would like to thank the inspirations for my poetry.

1. Love

One autumn morning,
He sits by the leaf-strewn porch in wonder,
Whether the human emotion of love,
Was a gift or the heart's sunder;

Was love a sunflower,
Waving and stretching out its face so bright,
Still longing for the delicate rays of the sun,
In the middle of the moonless night;

Was love an estranged young owl,
Who is stranded yonder at mid-day,
It flutters its wings with hope and intent,
With little regard to the sun's flay;

Was love a strife,
Of the dark blue ocean waves,
Searching aimlessly for the shore,
To at long last, finally, dig its own grave;

Was love a barren oak tree,
Longing for its foliage away an hour,
Bleeding care and shade,
To whoever may take shelter in it's bower;

His quest had ceased,
His mind had become allay,
He knew what love was,
When he saw her at the city bay.

2. An Ode To God

One's tenure of earthly sojourn,
Cessates as soon as it commences,
One reaches the threshold of heaven,
Before one can experience life's senses;

Why art thou so Vindictive,
Why art thou so Stubborn,
Thou steals the souls of many,
And prove to be an untimely burden;

Thou hath conceived from thy palms,
An Eden with grace and poise,
A haven for retreat and sanctuary,
For souls to merry and rejoice;

Thou art a deceiver,
Innocent souls are betrayed by thee,
They rise to heaven's doorways,
Under the Mirage of being free;

Thou must be ashamed of yourself,

Ridding fellows of a paradise,
Their refuge, their home,
For thou, nothing must suffice.

3. The Land Of The Gods

Where land is covered by mist till afar,
And shooting through yon are trees of fir and deodar,
Such is the land of Kashmir;

Where Snow-capped mountains rise above,
The clouds which are as white as a dove,
Such is the land of Kashmir;

Where flowers, orchids, and inflorescence bloom,
To impart color to our jewels,
Such is the land of Kashmir;

Where flora and fauna of all kinds grow,
Creating an illusion of the almighty's bestow,
Such is the land of Kashmir;

Where valleys, studded, as emeralds do,
 With lush and green form that hew,
Such is the land of Kashmir;

 Where crystal blue water graces the earth,
From snow caps that Bring it forth,
Such is the land of Kashmir;

Where people are true and kind,
Diversity reins with an open mind,
Such is the land of Kashmir;

Where nature interludes with humanity,
Both coexist with mutual perpetuity,
Such is the land of Kashmir;

The Land that we protect with iron rods,
The Land that belongs to the Gods,
Such is the land of Kashmir.

4. The Beauty Of The Earth

The beauty of the earth is unparalleled,
With features so great,
And mysteries yet to be unraveled,
Who will decide this world's fate;

The luscious green landscapes,
Spread across this wonder place,
Spreading an aura of serenity,
Putting a smile on every face;

The deep blue oceans,
Whose knowledge we have less,
The uncanny mysteries that unfold from within,
It glimmers wearing nature's dress;

The steep scenic highlands,
Spreading its reaches across the vast land,
Forming beautiful valleys and plains,
Turning the earth's ball grand;

But what are all these features,
Without anyone to appreciate them,
That's why God created us humans,
To be called " the earth's gems;"

But what are we humans doing,
To this gift, we have received,
We are harming it in unimaginable ways,
It's hard for it to be perceived;

Polluting this gift of humanity,
In all ways possible,
Without thinking for once,
If our attempts towards modernization are feasible;

This display of ungratefulness is intolerable,
Thus to spill my thoughts I am compelled,
I will say this now and I will say it forever,
The beauty of this earth is unparalleled.

5. Desolation

He was forsaken,
Near the cliff at the witch's hour,
By none than his lovers,
Who belonged to the myrtle's bower;

The Elysium burst out with tears,
With pours so great,
That caused torrent equivalent,
To that of Boecia's fate;

At that Twilight term,
He was a carcass without a soul,
Had a mind without thought,
With a heart filled with melancholy,
And eyes filled with naught;

Yon stranger approached,
From the dark verdure,
Gave counsel to the soul,
Who was stranded yonder askew;

He said "The fellows thou so love,
Ones for whom thou swain,
Doth they affect thou as much,

As fire does to rain;"

There was seldom to do,
But move on away,
To new lives and new companions,
Realizing the truth,
And treading on the path that lay.

6. One Day

A Day will come when.....
We will never sit together again breathing the same air,
We will never wave each other adieu in good and fair,
We will be oblivious to each other's highs and lows,
The classrooms will be filled with our silent echoes,
Our names scrawled on the benches will be the past,
For scribbled walls will forget our stories at last,
The teachers' pester will be left in the distant past,
The notes, submissions, and copies, will be gone at last,
The hallways will never be full of laughter again,
The school bell will never ring at ten,
The canteen will be filled with the ghosts of the past,
There will be no more selections for the annual day cast,
We will never again set foot in our second sanctuary,
Our hearts, for once, will be heavier than the bags that
we carry.

7. Journey Of Life

Looking out of the window of my car,
It dawned on my mind all of a sudden,
That the road is just like your life,
Brunting on other things burden;

The luscious mesmerizing mountains,
Smiling out with glee,
Brazen with wildlife and flora,
Feeling more than ever; free;

I continue this journey,
Through the breathtaking mountainous path,
Knowing whether or not,
It is full of happiness or Rath;

The view is so beautiful,
The valley is so calm,
I look over the horizon,
I get goosebumps over my palm;

Soon I reach a fork in the road,
Without knowing where the roads lead,
I take the one on the left,
Without knowing which one has what I need;

I reached a calm place,
Near the shore of the sea,
Thinking whether the journey was worth it,
And when I'll finally be filled with glee;

I would not know at once,
If this journey would be worth it or not,
As it was still not over,
Until the fuel runs out;

When after years and years to come,
When my car needs to mend,
I will understand that,
Finally, my time has come to an end;

I now look back at my journey,
Thinking about every moment in the past,
Looking back at the smiling mountains and noisy seas,
Knowing I have made the right choices,
Which lead me to where I am to be.

8. The Art Of Letting Go

In life, you must learn to lose,
For you can only grow,
If you have mastered,
The art of letting go;

The only thing permanent in life is impermanence,
The only constant is change,
The only thing stopping you from growing,
Is not striving beyond your range;

Your arms are only so wide,
Your grasp only chained,
By the ever-present you live in,
The only place you think you have gained;

But beware, my friend,
What pains the most,
Is stopping and not bidding adieu,
Before the memory becomes a haunting ghost,
And comes after you;

So let go, my friend,
Be free from the shambles of the past,

Reach new places in your journey,
For your time is ticking fast.

9. Vows

He said "I will never leave your side
Your wishes, I will truly abide,
I will hold your hand through land and sky
For my palms only need the grip of your love to sore
high
You are the reason I live and die for every moment of my
short life
You take my breath away every second that I am close to
you
You give me something to live for, something to wake up
out of bed for, something to fight for,
Know that if at all, you reach a point in life where no
one loves you anymore
Understand that I have been sentenced to death
By the jealous Gods who could not stand the existence of
such a heavenly bond.
If my love for you were to fit in a jar the size of the ever-
expanding universe,
It would still overflow, as rapidly as water would from a
flooded river
It is said that to love means to suffer if that is the case
My place on the planet would be to be the most
miserable man there is,
Such that suffering would be jealous of how much I

suffer for you,

I hope the world will end tomorrow. For our Love will be bonded forever in the records of time."

10. Conflict

O earth! Thou art everbearing,
Having set your loving arms over corpses ensnaring;

Thou art more crude than none,
None the humans that blaze with powder and gun;

I sympathize with thy battle-wounded, blood-washed, envious eye,
Be witness to brutality of mark so high;

For thy Cruor-soaked skin, I pray,
Let not tears of blooded pain flow astray;

O human! Why doth thou step foot on the land which hath thou borne,
That which reeps for the seeds of conflicts thou hath sown;

A demand laid forward by well-wishers speaks afar,
Halt thy ambition, and Halt thy mar.

11. Constance

O Constance, dare thou leave my side,
The world is ever so full of Hyde,
What surrounds me, deceives my sight,
Thou art chosen by my heart,
To understand my plight,
Thou art the constant in life, I pray,
Doth not be exposed to their sway,
O Constance, I fret thy absence,
A World with Thou less,
Pray I, Doth not wander into deceiving darkness,
O creator, thou hath made the world strange,
I ask, not but humbly, please removeth the change.

12. Fear of Failure

O world! O me!
Fret not by thy failure I say,
For tis not the end,
Doth not let thy mind sway;

Hath thou noticed in nature,
Shrubbery and Plants that grew neareth the earth, our mother,
Creepers that Slither on the Ground like Serpents,
Bear weighted food, on their stems, like none other;

They art afraid of failure,
Of not growing tall barks, branching leaves like tapestry,
But doth they halt and frown,
They let their follies be history;

O lord! O thee!
Trust not what the world says,
Channel thy fear of failure,
Push thy bounds,
Let thy ideas astray;

Like creepers doth bear,
Overtly large fruits and foods, burden the ground,

Foster the failure-shut gates of thy heart,
Open them to new notions,
In mind that is sound;

O fortune!
Doth not leave his side,
In eons and eons to come,
For it does not abandon,
The Heart of Conviction,
And the mind with a beating drum.

13. A Dream

I met someone today,

Someone who I could share with, my fears,
Someone who shed with me, my tears;

Someone who, for once in my life which was as bitter as
cider,
 Let me be the written, not the writer;

The Lord knows my heart's yearn,
Yet somehow she knew,
She impressed upon me a loved burn;

Oh my heart was put to shame, as if of little use,
For once, I was not the poet, I was the muse;

She was the one it undoubtedly seemed,
Into her heart, my soul gleamed;

Looking into her eyes, I saw a mirage,
A better me, a camouflage;

Oh heaven must be so jealous of me,
Wake Up boy, it's just a dream.;

It could never have been the reality,
Only a figment of my imagination in continuity.

14. New Times

O beloved!
I doth not blend in this age,
An age revered for infamy,
My conscience, akin a lion in a cage;

Around, with my eyes I see,
Matters which doth not concern me,
But why, oh why is such?
But why, oh why is such?

The beings living in this time,
Familiar, doth feel naught,
But again the query emerges,
Am I the human with a visage, they art not;

Doth all, leave me,
Have to live to live,
Or does life come caress their palms,
Like ignorance does, to a man begging for alms;

When with many, I am alone,
When myself I sit, I am with many,
Many of my thoughts, numerous perspectives,
Lord knows, who thinks the same, if any;

O beloved!
Doth not get swayed,
Like the wind, to a brow,
By these different beings,
For have I only thou.

15. Pandora's Box

A long Long time ago there was a decree,
About a box, sealed,
And under no circumstance,
Could the decree, ever be repealed;

It was buried in a far land,
Hidden in the forests deep,
Rumored to have as much treasure,
As one needs to fearfully sleep;

But some greedy men,
Sought out the riches-filled case,
Set out on the unknown land,
And disappeared without a trace,

The box was at last found,
And broken by it's chains and lock,
History remembered it as greed over law,
And the world remembered it as it's largest shock;

The case in question,
Was not an ordinary case at all,
 For it was a Hoax,
A curse in disguise,

It was the Pandora's Box;

The box was filled with,
What humans would make gore,
It was something children couldn't play with,
Nor should adults have,
It was war;

The effect of war spread over,
The vast stretch afar,
It hurt thousands and displaced millions,
Not without leaving a scar;

It affected men,
Drove their minds to slaughter
Their fellow brothers and God forbid,
They might return silent to their daughters;

The sad part about war,
It leaves none in its storm,
It torrents landscapes at large,
It rids us of the norm;

It affects all who can see it,
But more to the ones whose eyes yield,
Who wait in patience for years,
For their spouses to return,

From the battlefield;

How many times again,
Must for politicians, humans fall,
How much time before,
We will not have war at all;

Lord knows our fallacies,
Knows where we fall short,
He asks us to maintain peace,
But it is our choice,
Whether we want peace,
Or Soldier coffins' escort;

To whomsoever it may concern,
Putting a Stop to this game is the crux,
To this greedy game of war,
Put it back in the Pandora's Box.

16. The Grand Stage Of Life

As the grand stage of life,
Appears forth our doorfront,
Audition, a player, wish I,
Let thy actions be but blunt;

O life! What mysteries,
Thou hath hidden in thy unnoticed crevices,
All but selflessness shown by thee,
To let the present state be as can be;

O world! Let us embark,
On this odyssey told unto time,
To perform forth the audience,
As thespians, on the grand stage of life;

Doth thou please that,
Thy play go mild and plain,
Doth thou please that,
Thy works go to vain?

For, if no, then hear what I say,
Thy show will halt before open day,
If thou doth not understand,
Contribute an act, contribute a scene,

Contribute an emotion, contribute to the play.

17. Home

What mean by thou home?
Tis' a towering high rise in the middle of bustle?
Tis' a miniscule space for voices to echo?
Tis a spacious cottage at the edge?
Tis' a nomadic tent, with no present space?
Agree I should, with none,
Home is a place, thou art comfortable with,
An earth where events of thy interest hath chanced leave
second thought,
A place where thy day starts and halts,
A place that is thy last resort,
A place where thou sink in the blankets of thy emotion,
May it be in any form
A place that thou want to leave, and not come back
A place that thou want to come back, after leaving
Thus houses like tents, towers, spaces, and cottages,
They art not home, less they have thy heart,
Stored in the vaults of the ply and walls.

18. One in Many

Out of eight billion people in the world,
I met you;
Meeting you was finding a singular husk in the bag of
rice,
Except the husk was indifferent from the rest,
Yet somehow I was attracted to it,
Yet somehow I yearned for it in my dreams;
Somehow the poetry I wrote narrated itself when It
heard of you,
The songs composed themselves,
The flowers bloomed by themselves,
And my heart,
My heart emptied the blood flowing through its rugged,
old passages,
To accommodate the love that I felt for you.

19. Misunderstanding

It was only a misunderstanding after all,
Years of friendship, years of love,
All depending on just one fabric,
A fabric that can be broken, not by the sharpest of
swords,
But the most blunt words,
The most blunt words understood differently,
Misinterpreted meanings and understandings,
It may be love disguised as hatred,
Or anger disguised as irony,
How broken can one's heart be,
If he lost people due to misunderstandings,
It was not their fault yet it was understood to be,
It was not their mistake, just fate which resulted in the
change of perspective to a thought,
It was merely a misunderstanding.

20. कशी

भारत की दिव्य भूमी में,
सबसे दिव्य है कशी;
ब्रम्ह-वध करने वाले महाकाल,
को बारह वर्ष के आदि, यहाँ मिली क्षमा;
जहा मणिकर्णिका के तट से, निराकार भटकती आत्मा,
जहा जन्म से अधिक मौत का जश्न मनाया जाय;
जहा मृत्य व्यक्ति की अस्थि,
दे अघोरियों की जीवन शक्ति;
मोक्ष प्राप्ति की ओर चले मुसाफिर कशी,
काल भैरव के चरण स्पर्श करने चले कशी;
दुनिया ख़तम हो जाएगी, संसार ख़तम हो जायेगा,
पर रहेगा तोह सिर्फ शिव शम्भू का राज्य;
हे कशी ! ओ कशी !

21. End of an Era

It is only a matter of time,
Before this all comes to an end,
The laughter, the joy, the good times,
It lasted for years,
Years which now feel like the end of a song,
But sadly, it cannot be replayed like one,
These were the best moments of the short life i have
lived,
Memories to be cherished in the future,
Stories for the next generation,
Oh what a Time !
This is the end of an era.

www.ingramcontent.com/pod-product-compliance
Lightning Source LLC
La Vergne TN
LVHW010831200726
843508LV00012B/2560